Susan Derech

THE
Responsibility
RULES

Leading a Self-Disciplined Life
in a Self-Entitled World

Susan Dench

The Responsibility Rules:
Living a Self-Disciplined Life in a Self-Entitled World
Susan Dench

Contact us at:
Muddy Dog Media
295 Foreside Road
Falmouth, Maine 04015
207.899.0301
susan@susandench.com

ISBN 10: 0984751807
ISBN 13: 978-0-9847518-0-8

Book Design: www.KarrieRoss.com

DEDICATION

This book is lovingly dedicated to my
parents, Sidney and Gillian Woodcock,
who taught me the Responsibility Rules
by living them every day, and to my
darling husband, Bryan, and our
combined crew of children –
Elisabeth, Bret and Beatrice, Joe,
Charlotte, Allison and Sarah – for whom
I hope I do the same.

SO LIVE THAT
YOU WOULDN'T
BE ASHAMED TO SELL
THE FAMILY PARROT
TO THE TOWN GOSSIP.

—WILL ROGERS

Introduction

A mediocre soccer player whines that he isn't getting enough playing time and the (volunteer) coach is harassed by the parents to get him out on the field. The parents of a high schooler swoop in to have bullying words with the headmaster because their child didn't get an A in a class, and the grade is indeed changed after a not-so-subtle parental reminder that the child's grandparents donated a wing to the school. A newly minted lawyer is disgruntled and sullen because she isn't receiving daily kudos and recognition for the fabulous work she mistakenly thinks she is doing. A criminal gets away with a slap on the wrist because he has shown remorse and the judge feels his miserable childhood should excuse his illicit behavior. An uninsured patient shrieks at a harried Emergency Department nurse that health care is his "right" and she had better get cracking. And my all-time personal favorite: the Detroit woman who talked about getting "Obama money" (that is, stimulus money and therefore, my tax money) from "his stash." Sadly, these are all true stories, and I bet we all have many more examples of our own to add.

What is going on here?! Why have self-discipline, manners, civility and personal responsibility seemingly become obsolete, and when did self-entitlement become epidemic? With an over-developed sense of unearned privilege, there is no responsibility taken for personal actions and mistakes, and a pervasive expectation that someone else will always be there to take care of any pesky situations that may arise without any bother or expense to the "victim." And while the "victim" shows no regard or concern for anyone around him, he vigorously defends what he perceives to be his.

We can't imagine what some of these parents think they are teaching their children about personal responsibility, respect – for themselves and those in authority, about earning something by merit, about integrity. No wonder so many twenty-somethings need to be constantly reassured that they are doing a great job at work – because we don't keep score on the younger sports teams for fear of offending the less talented teams/ players (although most kids with an ounce of intrinsic competitive spirit can tell you exactly what the score actually was), because we tell them what a great job they did even if they played or performed horribly (which they are already acutely aware of as they come off the field), because we give them trophies just for showing up, because we think that just because we complain about something, teachers/coaches should hop to and accede to our demands.

We make such a fuss over them that as they get older, kids seem to be screaming for continued attention through the use of Twitter, Facebook status updates and blogs, making sure that they are "followed" or "liked" by as many fans as possible. Outstanding achievement isn't acknowledged or recognized so no child's "self-esteem" is compromised, and mediocrity becomes the standard to which kids aspire. Anything given is simply taken for granted.

Our children are becoming soft and narcissistic with an overly enhanced sense of self-esteem, can't cope with the "real world" and have unrealistic expectations of what life "owes" them. Conspicuous consumerism and instant gratification run rampant.

Jeffrey Zaslow's Wall Street Journal piece about large companies such as Lands' End and Bank of America hiring consultants to teach managers to keep up with younger employees' insatiable need for praise and demand for positive reinforcement – basically forming "praise teams" – was stunning in its commentary on how low we've sunk. I mean, they're kidding, right? The boss is supposed to spend precious previously productive working hours actually rhapsodizing poetic about the accomplishments – or not – of his young charges? And while we might read about the PR-spun success of these manufactured celebratory tactics (being a marketer, I know how this stuff works), we're never quite told how they drive improved performance.

Exactly what happened to the pursuit of excellence and the just reward for hard work and talent? What happened to allowing our children to develop character, moral fiber, fortitude?

And this shift isn't merely generational: It appears to be pervasive societally.

To our great detriment, standards, structure and values have become relaxed to the point where there are no rules, no punishment for bad behavior, no consequences for adverse actions. Instead we are becoming a nation of self-entitled, victim-mentality wussies, devaluing excellence in the name of political correctness and feminizing our boys and men away from the natural roles they should play in society. (Yes, that is another book.) Entitlement and self-centeredness are curses. Self-indulgence is over-rated, a spiritual dead end. These characteristics doom one to a life of misery because one cannot bear any criticism, be empathetic to others or do anything that places others' needs above their own. Under these societal norms, it's really no wonder that so many marriages fail.

How do we get back on the right track? We need to reimpose structure and standards, extolling and celebrating the value of self-discipline, which in turn provides a self-supporting, responsible society. That means doing the right thing when our friends or colleagues are beckoning us to do otherwise. That means standing fast and not taking the easy, but most expedient, way out. That means hanging tough as parents, knowing that we are not going to be liked all the time and remembering that we actually are parents, not our childrens' friends. We should live like we would be proud to have our actions posted on the front page of the newspaper – above the fold.

So how do we develop self-discipline? It's been said that if something is done for 30 consecutive days it becomes a habit. Making self-discipline a habit may mean taking small, incremental steps until it becomes as natural as breathing. Once you take responsibility for a situation, you can take control, and taking back control of your circumstance is actually incredibly empowering, allowing you to set the agenda and tackle any challenge. And the more you impose self-discipline and integrate it into your everyday life, the faster you'll be able to reach your goals. The more you do it, the easier it will become. Start with small victories and work your way up. Kids live up – or down – to our expectations so parents should give them something to aspire to, starting at home. And when you want to give up, ask God for His help. You can't go wrong there.

Practicing personal responsibility, self-discipline, accountability, courtesy and respect everyday is challenging and very difficult. They all require courage.

The 10 Commandments weren't given as the 10 Suggestions.

Rules are made for a reason. Some are meant to be broken, but the Responsibility Rules are not.

Aristotle said, "Excellence is an art won by training and habituation. We do not act rightly because we have virtue or excellence, but we rather have those because we have acted rightly. We are what we repeatedly do. Excellence, then, is not an act but a habit."

Pearl Buck said, "We need to restore the full meaning of that old word, duty. It is the other side of rights."

What would your parrot say?

THE
Responsibility
RULES

RULE 1:

Do unto others as you would have done unto you

"Never, never be afraid to do what's right, especially if the well-being of a person or animal is at stake. Society's punishments are small compared to the wounds we inflict on our soul when we look the other way."

—Martin Luther King Jr.

Rule 2:
You have a right to the pursuit
of happiness, not happiness itself

Rule 3:
Develop a strong work ethic

Rule 4:
Remember that you may not be able to
control what happens to you, but you can
control your reaction to it

*"Practice mercy and justice and
walk humbly with your God."*

—Micah 6:8

RULE 5:
Strive for excellence in all you do

RULE 6:
Learn to give a firm handshake and rise when someone enters a room

RULE 7:
Make learning new things a lifelong habit

*"I never look at the masses as my
responsibility; I look at the individual.
I can only love one person at a time – just
one, one, one. So you begin. I began –
I picked up one person. Maybe if I didn't pick
up that one person, I wouldn't have picked up
forty-two thousand....The same thing goes for
you, the same thing in your family, the same
thing in your church, your community.
Just begin – one, one, one."*

—Mother Teresa of Calcutta

Rule 8:
Take responsibility for your actions,
good or bad

Rule 9:
No texting while driving, please, and if
you have to be on the phone, use your
hands-free feature

Rule 10:
Read more books and brush
up on Shakespeare and the classics –
your horizons will widen

"Always do right. This will gratify some people and astonish the rest."

—Mark Twain

RULE 11:

Say your prayers and be profoundly thankful for all God has given you

*"Freedom is the will to be responsible
to ourselves."*

—Friedrich Nietzsche

RULE 12:
It's true – life isn't fair

RULE 13:
School may have abolished winners
and losers, but life hasn't

RULE 14:
Challenge yourself and stray
outside your comfort zone every
now and then

"I believe that every right implies a responsibility; every opportunity, an obligation; every possession, a duty."

—John D. Rockefeller, Jr.

RULE 15:

You don't get a medal for just showing up – healthy self-esteem is derived through hard work and accomplishments

"We have the Bill of Rights.
What we need is a Bill of Responsibilities."

—Bill Maher

RULE 16:
Get to bed on time and remember that the early bird catches the worm

RULE 17:
Carpe diem (if you don't know what that means, learn a little Latin)

RULE 18:
Don't let your mail pile up and pay your bills on time

"Take your life in your own hands, and what happens? A terrible thing: No one to blame."

—Erica Jong

RULE 19:
Eat your vegetables

RULE 20:
You will not earn six figures, have a corner office, be able to join the right club and afford a McMansion just out of high school (or probably just out of college either)

RULE 21:
Look both ways –
and not just on the street

"Responsibility is the price of greatness."

—Winston Churchill

RULE 22:
Do not interrupt

RULE 23:
Wash your hands after using the bathroom and before eating

RULE 24:
Make your bed every morning

RULE 25:
Know the difference between want and need

"The willingness to accept responsibility for one's own life is the source from which self-respect springs."

—Joan Didion

RULE 26:
Sometimes it's okay to
eat dessert first

RULE 27:
Discipline is not the same
as punishment

RULE 28:
When you make a cake it's okay to
lick the spoon

"We need to restore the full meaning of that old word, duty. It is the other side of rights."

—Pearl Buck

RULE 29:
Limit computer time

RULE 30:
Always say "please" and "thank you" and send a "thank you" note when you have received a kindness

RULE 31:
Remember that you'll get more flies with honey than with vinegar

"She was the archetypal selfless mother: living only for her children, sheltering them from the consequences of their actions — and in the end doing them irreparable harm."

—Marcia Muller

RULE 32:

Hold the door open for the next person
(this has nothing to do with gender and
everything to do with civility)

RULE 33:

The role of the government is keeping you
safe, not giving you handouts – and if you
think that having the government provide
for you and making your
decisions is all right, realize that you
have also given up the freedom that
comes with free choice

RULE 34:

Smile a lot – people are drawn to
a happy demeanor and it'll make you feel
better as well

Rule 35:

Don't do it because you have to; do it because you want to

RULE 36:
Use your coupons before they expire

RULE 37:
Get a good education – no matter what happens, that knowledge will always remain

RULE 38:
Make lists for chores and goals and stick to them

"Ninety-nine percent of all failures come from people who have a habit of making excuses."

—George Washington Carver

Rule 39:
Follow through and follow up

Rule 40:
Feed the meter

Rule 41:
Welcome the new neighbors with a list of all the places they'll need and may not know: bakery, lawn care, dry cleaners, repair man, cleaning service, etc.

"It is the responsibility of leadership to provide opportunity, and the responsibility of individuals to contribute."

—William Pollard

RULE 42:
Be a gracious winner and loser

RULE 43:
Always clean up after your dog

RULE 44:
Use the gifts God gave you

RULE 45:
Count to 10 before you say something
you might regret

"We are apt to forget that children watch examples better than they listen to preaching."

—Roy L. Smith

RULE 46:
Don't complain – use the word
"opportunity" instead of "problem"

RULE 47:
Get some exercise every day

RULE 48:
Do not judge, but exercise discernment
after you have all the facts, otherwise you
can never act on what you know and
believe to be right

"A man does what he must - in spite of personal consequences, in spite of obstacles and dangers and pressures – and that is the basis of all human morality."

—Winston Churchill

RULE 49:
Take time to take care of yourself –
there's a reason they have you put
the oxygen mask on yourself
before others

RULE 50:
Return phone calls, work or personal,
within 24 hours

RULE 51:
Do not talk on a cell phone in public

"I am free because I know that I alone am morally responsible for everything I do."

—Robert A. Heinlein

RULE 52:
Be kind even when it's hard

RULE 53:
Use it up, wear it out, make it do or do without

RULE 54:
Stay true to yourself

RULE 55:

Don't do or post anything you wouldn't want seen on the front page of the newspaper

RULE 56:

Keep all your important papers organized

RULE 57:

Don't talk at the movies

RULE 58:

Admit when you are wrong and
look someone in the eye when
you say, "I am sorry"

*"It is one thing to show your child the way,
and a harder thing to then stand out of it."*

—Robert Brault

RULE 59:
Say "excuse me" when you need to

RULE 60:
Remember that whatever you do will leave a mark

RULE 61:
Practice good sportsmanship on the field

"Life is a gift, and it offers us the privilege, opportunity, and responsibility to give something back by becoming more."

—Anthony Robbins

RULE 62:

Don't cheer at opponents' missed shots

RULE 63:

Don't let other people's actions dictate
your own

RULE 64:

Stand up straight and don't slouch

"If you want children to keep their feet on the ground, put some responsibility on their shoulders."

—Abigail Van Buren

RULE 65:
Take care of your possessions

RULE 66:
Try to hold a family mealtime

RULE 67:
Donate to and volunteer for a cause about which you are passionate

"Today, more than ever before, life must be characterized by a sense of universal responsibility, not only nation to nation and human to human, but also human to other forms of life."

—Dalai Lama

RULE 68:
Ladies, in business and in social situations you should be willing to extend your hand first

RULE 69:
Remember — everything in moderation

RULE 70:
Live your life with no regrets

RULE 71:
Send a handwritten note to someone just because

*"Live so that when your children think of
fairness and integrity, they think of you."*

—H. Jackson Brown

RULE 72:

Develop and use your sense of
humor – frequently

RULE 73:

Remember that the host/hostess sets the
mood for his/her event – if you aren't having fun, neither are your guests

RULE 74:

Take pride in how you look, speak, and
interact with society

"If you tell the truth, you don't have to remember anything."

—Mark Twain

RULE 75:
Pick up after yourself and don't leave your rubbish for somebody else

RULE 76:
Keep your elbows off the table, chew with your mouth closed, take small bites of food and don't talk with your mouth full

RULE 77:
Dress for the job you want, not the job you have

"In the old days, words like sin and Satan had a moral certitude. Today, they're replaced with self-help jargon, words like dysfunction and antisocial behavior, discouraging any responsibility for one's actions."

—Don Henley

RULE 78:
Be kind and generous in spirit

RULE 79:
Buy and use an etiquette book

RULE 80:
Floss and put the cap on the toothpaste

"A chief is a man who assumes responsibility. He says 'I was beaten,' he does not say 'My men were beaten'."

—Antoine de Saint-Exupery

RULE 81:
Never cut in line (and if someone has been kind enough to open the door and let you in ahead of him, let him go before you in line)

RULE 82:
Take the high road (the low road is too crowded) and practice discretion

RULE 83:

Praise in public, discipline in private

RULE 84:
Spend within or below your means

RULE 85:
Save voraciously

RULE 86:
Put your best foot forward

*"Liberty means responsibility.
That is why most men dread it."*

—George Bernard Shaw

RULE 87:
Observe and obey the speed limit

RULE 88:
Reduce, reuse, recycle

RULE 89:
Tell those you love every day that you love them

*"The school will teach children how
to read, but the environment of the home
must teach them what to read. The school
can teach them how to think, but the home
must teach them what to believe."*

—Charles A. Wells

RULE 90:
Give credit where credit is due

RULE 91:
As they say at Harvard, fight fiercely

RULE 92:
Live simply and practice modesty

*"My father didn't tell me how to live,
he lived, and let me watch him do it."*

—Clarence Budinton Kelland

RULE 93:
Respect your elders

RULE 94:
Practice restraint and self-control

RULE 95:
Be honest with yourself

*"Power without responsibility –
the prerogative of the harlot throughout
the ages."*

—Rudyard Kipling

RULE 96:
Take your vitamins

RULE 97:
Take time to smell the flowers

RULE 98:
Return everything you borrow

RULE 99:
Pay it forward – if someone has no change for the parking meter, step in and help him out

"We need to stop the erosion of parental authority."

—Sonny Landham

RULE 100:
Make and keep those doctor and dental appointments

RULE 101:
Don't procrastinate

RULE 102:
Have the courage to make unpopular decisions when you know they are right

RULE 103:
Have the courage of your convictions and stand for something

"Don't worry that children never listen to you;
worry that they are always watching you."

—Robert Fulghum

RULE 104:

Forgive yourself – hindsite provides 20/20 vision, so don't beat yourself up over a decision that seemed right when you made it

RULE 105:

Persevere when the going gets tough – loss happens but life goes on

RULE 106:

Have compassion, especially for those not as fortunate as yourself

*"When government accepts responsibility
for people, then people no longer take
responsibility for themselves."*

—George Pataki

RULE 107:
Dont hold a grudge – it takes too much energy

RULE 108:
Be trustworthy – your reputation and your name are invaluable

RULE 109:
Be tactful and tell someone something about their appearance only if they can do something about it right then

RULE 110:

Be honorable in all
your dealings – your name
and your reputation are
invaluable

RULE 111:

Always wear your seat belt

RULE 112:

Find and act on your passion

RULE 113:

Forgive those who sin against you

"I try to live what I consider a 'poetic existence.' That means I take responsibility for the air I breathe and the space I take up. I try to be immediate, to be totally present for all my work."

—Maya Angelou

RULE 114:
Remember that beauty is in the eye
of the beholder

RULE 115:
Look for the good in people and give
them the benefit of the doubt

RULE 116:
Change can be scary, but it can also be
exciting

"We are alone, with no excuses.
That is the idea I shall try to convey
when I say that man is condemned to be free.
Condemned, because he did not create
himself, yet, in other respects is free;
because, once thrown into the world, he is
responsible for everything he does."

—Jean-Paul Sartre

RULE 117:
Be a loyal friend and spouse, in good
times and bad

RULE 118:
Stop thinking negatively – it can become
a self-fulfilling prophecy

RULE 119:
Keep your word – if you say you are going
to do something, do it

*"People think responsibility is hard to bear.
It's not. I think that sometimes it is the
absence of responsibility that is harder to
bear. You have a great feeling of impotence."*

—Henry Kissinger

RULE 120:
Under promise and over deliver

RULE 121:
Remember that God loves you so you're never alone and no trouble is beyond help

RULE 122:
Yesterday is gone – live for today

*"To bring up a child in the way he should go,
travel that way yourself once in a while."*

—Josh Billings

RULE 123:
Question with boldness and with sincerity

RULE 124:
Arrogance is a singularly unattractive characteristic

RULE 125:
Look for the exits

*"You can delegate authority, but
not responsibility."*

—Stephen W. Comiskey

RULE 126:
Respect all living creatures

RULE 127:
Remember that every time you leave the
house, your family name follows you

RULE 128:
Marry for love and for laughter
but marry for God

"The first responsibility of a leader is to define reality. The last is to say thank you. In between, the leader is a servant."

—Max De Pree

RULE 129:
Know that material stuff doesn't matter in the scheme of things

RULE 130:
Remember that even a bad experience can be used to shape your life

RULE 131:
Call 911 first

"Success is not final, failure is not fatal: it is the courage to continue that counts."

—Winston Churchill

Rule 132:

Always have a picture on your desk
of someone you love and someone
you admire

Rule 133:

Keep your shoes polished

Rule 134:

Choose who you are otherwise other
people will define you

Rule 135:

Before visiting a foreign country, read up
about its history, politics and culture and
at least try to speak a few words of the
local language

RULE 136:

Remember that your job is what you do, not who you are

RULE 137:
No pain, no gain

RULE 138:
If it is appropriate, ask, because if you don't ask, you don't get

RULE 139:
The biggest rewards come from the biggest risks

"'I must do something' always solves more problems than 'Something must be done.'"

—Author Unknown

RULE 140:
Life is hard – and then it gets harder

RULE 141:
Fool me once, shame on you: Fool me twice, shame on me

RULE 142:
Our freedom and rights are given to man by God – but we must do everything to protect them

Rule 143:

Vote – the right to do so is something for which many heroes have devoted and given their lives

RULE 144:
Remember that your work is a portrait of yourself

RULE 145:
Respect your parents even when you disagree with them

RULE 146:
Wear your pearls, and use your crystal and best china – there's no point in having beautiful things and not using them

"You are responsible, forever,
for what you have tamed.
You are responsible for your rose."

—Antoine de Saint-Exupery

RULE 147:
Walk a lot and smell the roses as you go

RULE 148:
There are no coincidences

RULE 149:
Never want anything too much, there will be too high a price to pay

RULE 150:
If you have to shoot, shoot to kill

Rule 151:

Don't let the sun go down while you are angry

RULE 152:
Stand up straight

RULE 153:
It's not what you say, it's how you say it – remember that "a quiet word turns away anger"

RULE 154:
Cherish your friends, and realize they will come and go

RULE 155:
The hardest thing to do is admit failure and weakness, but to do so shows strength

*"Be judicious about who you surround
yourself with. Hire people, engage people who
are smarter than you are, and who are happy
in their own skin. Stay away from angry
people, people who feel like they've been
misused. Attitude is far more important than
demonstrated skill, because that skill can be
taught if there's a willing attitude. The other
thing that goes with that is, give people
freedom to make mistakes. Because,
ultimately, it's only through mistakes
that we learn."*

—Tom Moser

RULE 156:
Keep your car clean

RULE 157:
Enunciate your words and don't mumble

RULE 158:
Develop a broad vocabulary – it will help
you to think more clearly

RULE 159:
Use good grammar in speech and
in writing

*"Life affords no greater responsibility,
no greater privilege, than the raising
of the next generation."*

—C. Everett Koop

RULE 160:
Don't worry about brand names –
purchase what provides the best value

RULE 161:
Wash and put away the dishes as
they get dirty

RULE 162:
Your vocabulary is probably big
enough to preclude swearing
(and taking God's name in vain)

RULE 163:
A positive attitude and enthusiasm
are contagious

"A man sooner or later discovers that he is the master-gardener of his soul, the director of his life."

—James Allen

RULE 164:

Don't expect someone to come in and clean up your messes for you

RULE 165:

Do what you love, the money will follow

RULE 166:

Wear a name tag (on the right side so it's easier to read when shaking hands)

RULE 167:

Adapt and change when needed

"If you mess up, 'fess up."

—Author Unknown

RULE 168:
Don't hide your light under a bushel

RULE 169:
Trust your gut intuition and follow
your instincts

RULE 170:
Adult children should not live at home

RULE 171:
Don't let others make decisions for you –
there's only one person who determines
your destiny, and that's you

"'It's a question of discipline,' the little prince told me later on. 'When you've finished washing and dressing each morning, you must tend your planet.'"

—Antoine de Saint-Exupéry,
The Little Prince

RULE 172:
Hang up your clothes and put away the laundry

RULE 173:
There's a reason it's called "work"

RULE 174:
Be respectful of others and be on time for appointments

RULE 175:
The parents' job is to make themselves obsolete

"Responsibility: A detachable burden easily shifted to the shoulders of God, Fate, Fortune, Luck or one's neighbor. In the days of astrology it was customary to unload it upon a star."

—Ambrose Bierce,
The Devil's Dictionary

RULE 176:
Lead by example

RULE 177:
Stand for the national anthem and men – take your hat off and place it over your heart, women – put your hand over your heart

RULE 178:
Drink responsibly and don't drink at an office function

RULE 179:
When you see an individual in a military uniform, thank them for their service and perhaps buy them a cup of coffee or a meal (anonymously if you can)

RULE 180:

Learn civics

RULE 181:

Visualize your goals – once a year write them down and focus on accomplishing them

RULE 182:

Be kind to the help

RULE 183:

Avoid working with jerks – it takes up too much time and energy

"Responsibility's like a string we can only see the middle of. Both ends are out of sight."

—William McFee,
Casuals of the Sea

RULE 184:
Always be thinking of how you can accomplish things economically

RULE 185:
Keep track of your money and invest at an early age (although it's never too late to start)

RULE 189:
Hire people smarter than you

RULE 190:
You will be judged by the company you keep

"Most of us can read the writing on the wall; we just assume it's addressed to someone else."

—Ivern Ball

RULE 191:

Know and respect your personal limits

RULE 192:

You are allowed to change your mind

RULE 193:

Make friends with those who think differently from you, and across the age spectrum

RULE 194:

If requested, RSVP promptly

RULE 195:

Ask for help if you need it

RULE 196:
Bigger forces are not working against you – you are the only one working against you

RULE 197:
Give reasons, not excuses and blame

RULE 198:
You're not perfect, and it's no one else's fault you're not perfect

RULE 199:
Read and understand what you're signing – the big print giveth, but the small print can taketh away

"The great thought, the great concern, the great anxiety of men is to restrict, as much as possible, the limits of their own responsibility."

—Giosué Borsi

RULE 200:
Adult children should not be on the parental dole

RULE 201:
When you find yourself in a hole, stop digging

RULE 202:
Don't throw good money after bad

RULE 203:
There is no such thing as a free lunch, someone is paying for it

*"Being responsible sometimes means
pissing people off."*

—Colin Powell

RULE 204:

Get your next pet from the animal shelter

RULE 205:

If something is too good to be true, it probably is

RULE 206:

Show respect for teachers, police officers and firefighters

RULE 207:

Don't believe everything you read/hear

Rule 208:

Trust but verify

RULE 209:

Let another driver pull ahead of you when
you're stopped in traffic

RULE 210:

Demand excellence –
and expect to pay for it

RULE 211:

Never invest more in the stock market
than you can afford to lose

*"If it's your job to eat a frog, it's best
to do it first thing in the morning.
And if it's your job to eat two frogs,
it's best to eat the biggest one first."*

—Mark Twain

Rule 212:
Be an original thinker

Rule 213:
Make an effort to learn – and use – people's names

Rule 214:
Never make an important decision without sleeping on it

Rule 215:
Instead of telling people how to do something, tell them what needs to be done

"Ef you take a sword an' dror it,
An' go stick a feller thru,
Guv'ment ain't to answer for it,
God'll send the bill to you."

—James Russell Lowell

Rule 216:

Be proactive, not reactive

Rule 217:

Keep a journal, as life goes by too fast

Rule 218:

Never cheat – on anything or anyone

Rule 219:

Don't discuss important or confidential
things in public – the walls have ears

*"Even when we know what is right,
too often we fail to act. More often we grab
greedily for the day, letting tomorrow
bring what it will, putting off the unpleasant
and unpopular."*

—Bernard M. Baruch

RULE 220:

Tip generously for all service and more generously for outstanding service, but don't compensate and encourage subpar performance (and good managers will want to know about your experience)

RULE 221:

Become a mentor

RULE 222:

No one ever wished on his death bed that he had spent more time in the office

"The best years of your life are the ones in which you decide your problems are your own. You do not blame them on your mother, the ecology, or the president. You realize that you control your own destiny."

—Albert Ellis

RULE 223:
Politicians work for you, so don't be afraid to call or write to let them know how you feel

RULE 224:
If you have a superior customer service experience, write to the person in charge and compliment his/her staff

RULE 225:
You never get a second chance to make a first impression

"Man must cease attributing his problems to his environment, and learn again to exercise his will – his personal responsibility."

—Albert Einstein

RULE 226:
It's okay to disagree,
but disagree respectfully

RULE 227:
If someone criticizes what you are doing,
instead of being defensive, stop and think
about it. The criticism may be warranted
and you might learn something from it

RULE 228:
Busyness does not equal performance

"Why do children want to grow up?
Because they experience their lives
as constrained by immaturity and perceive
adulthood as a condition of greater freedom
and opportunity. But what is there today, in
America, that very poor and very rich
adolescents want to do but cannot do?
Not much: They can 'do' drugs, 'have'
sex, 'make' babies, and 'get' money (from
their parents, crime, or the State).
For such adolescents, adulthood becomes
synonymous with responsibility rather
than liberty. Is it any surprise that they
remain adolescents?"

—Thomas Szasz

RULE 229:

Call your mother

*"With every civil right there has to be
a corresponding civil obligation."*

—Edison Haines

Homework

If you don't know where you're going, you're never going to get there. So now you have the Rules, get moving!

Remember Rule 38 regarding writing down your goals? If you want to really develop self-discipline, start by developing goals, and then actually writing them down. Think positively and phrase things in terms of what you want to accomplish, moving forward toward a goal.

By seeing your goals on paper:

- You have a written contract with yourself
- You have clearly stated just what you want to achieve

The next steps are:

- Making sure your goals are detailed and specific so you know precisely what it is you want to achieve
- Developing plans outlining how you will achieve your objectives
- Adding realistic milestones and deadlines to your goals

Try to limit the number of goals you want to achieve to 3 or 4 so you don't feel overwhelmed.

Make some goals easier to reach and develop some "stretch" goals which you know will require more work.

Review your goals often and revise as necessary – and remember that revising doesn't mean something hasn't worked, it means that you are using your insights to reset.

Do something every day to work toward achieving your goals.

Visualize yourself reaching your goal - you might even want to use images of various people, places or things to motivate you.

Following the Responsibility Rules is tough, but achieving personal goals through your own hard work and discipline will empower you, liberate you and give you confidence to accomplish all that you want to in life.

Your parrot will be proud.

About The Author

Susan Dench knows that even though her job as a mother is to make herself obsolete, she will always worry about her children. As they will be only too happy to confirm, she is never afraid to give her opinion if asked (and usually if not asked). Susan has several different subjects about which she is absolutely passionate—helping organizations get smart about connecting with their clients through her company, Muddy Dog Media; inspiring women who want to succeed in whatever personal or professional adventure they've chosen; and injecting responsibility and accountability into our culture by spreading the word on the Power of Personal Responsibility. She lives on the coast of Maine with her exceedingly indulgent husband and admittedly spoiled pets in a charming 1920's house, which is in a perpetual state of renovation. She can be found at susandench.com or reached at susan@susandench.com.

"The ultimate folly is to think that something crucial to your welfare is being taken care of for you."

—Robert Brault